DESPERATE FOR CHANGE

DESPERATE
FOR CHANGE

By
Kim Cornell

XULON PRESS

Xulon Press
2301 Lucien Way #415
Maitland, FL 32751
407.339.4217
www.xulonpress.com

© 2022 by Kim Cornell

All rights reserved solely by the author. The author guarantees all contents are original and do not infringe upon the legal rights of any other person or work. No part of this book may be reproduced in any form without the permission of the author.

Due to the changing nature of the Internet, if there are any web addresses, links, or URLs included in this manuscript, these may have been altered and may no longer be accessible. The views and opinions shared in this book belong solely to the author and do not necessarily reflect those of the publisher. The publisher therefore disclaims responsibility for the views or opinions expressed within the work.

Unless otherwise indicated, Scripture quotations taken from the King James Version (KJV) – *public domain.*

Scripture quotations taken from the Holy Bible, New International Version (NIV). Copyright © 1973, 1978, 1984, 2011 by Biblica, Inc.™. Used by permission. All rights reserved.

Paperback ISBN-13: 978-1-66286-572-5
Ebook ISBN-13: 978-1-66286-573-2

CONTENTS

CHAPTER 1
Acceptance
Pg. 1

CHAPTER 2
Repentance
Pg. 9

CHAPTER 3
Forgiveness
Pg. 17

CHAPTER 4
Healing the Soul
Pg. 23

CHAPTER 5
Freedom
Pg. 27

I dedicate this book
to all those who are incarcerated,
especially QD0049

FROM THE AUTHOR

Are you looking for real change in your life? Are you tired of living a life of misery and hopelessness? How desperate are you for this change? Because the only way you will get real change in your life is to be desperate for change and ready to take extreme measures.

To get from prison to true freedom is going to be a process. You have to say to yourself, okay, I'm in this prison and I desperately want to get out and stay out. I'll do whatever it takes.

Well, if you have that mindset, then this book will take you through all the steps you need to take to get there.

When you read this book, you may not like what you read. It's going to be the hard truth, in your face, that you may have been hiding from.

You might say, "No, I can't do that."

I say, "Yes, you can if you are desperate for change.

Desperate for your freedom…"

Prison – A building in which people are legally held as a punishment for a crime they have committed

Freedom – The power or right to act, speak or think as one wants without hindrance or restraint.

Chapter 1
ACCEPTANCE

To get from Prison to Freedom is going to take some work. Especially if you want real freedom. I don't mean just freedom from prison to the streets. I mean true freedom. You may be getting ready to be released from your physical prison that you're incarcerated in, but you also must be set free from your mental prison that you're also doing time in, or you'll be coming right back.

Yes, you are also being held in a mental prison whether you realize it or not. Your mental prison is created by sin, negative thinking, wrong thoughts, false truths, wrong attitudes. How do I know that you're mentally imprisoned? Because you're here. Your mental prison has led you to living in a physical prison.

Think about it, why are you here? You're here because you broke the law. Not because you got caught, but because you broke the law. Some people think it's okay to break the law as long as you don't get caught. Which is not the right way of thinking. And that's one of the reasons you can be in a mental prison because you're not thinking right. Why aren't you thinking right? Usually, it's caused from an event or series of events that bring trauma into a person's life. Whether it was abuse, abandonment, a loved one dying, some kind of tragedy that happened to you along life's journey. It causes something to be broken inside of you and your thinking is changed. Instead of thinking rationally, you adapt a new way of thinking to cope with all the hurt, pain, and suffering you're going through.

Now again, why are you here? Because you broke the law. Accept the fact that you broke the law, and this is your punishment. To stay out of prison you must not break the law.

Now, let's try to get your mind right again. Let's start from the beginning, were you born into a loving home with two loving parents who had it all together? That's not the case for most who end up here. Were you born into Poverty? Dysfunction? An absent parent that wasn't there when you were born? Or maybe left later in life? No matter what scenario you were born into, it all started when you were in your mother's womb.

Your parent's decisions carved out your path to birth. So, if you were born poor, in the projects, into a house of dysfunction. It was your parent's fault. Their decisions in their life,

ACCEPTANCE

before you were born, carved out the path to the environment you were birthed into.

But don't blame them, maybe their parents did the same thing to them. And maybe your grandparent's parents, did the same thing to them. Well, that becomes a generational curse until a generation finally stops it.

So back to your beginning. Yes, your parents were responsible for what you were born into but after that, it's all you. We are all taught good vs evil at some point in our lives. Whether it was your parents, teachers, or society, you were taught right from wrong. It was even built right into your body, called your conscience. God put within each of us, a conscience.

> **Conscience** – *An inner feeling or voice acting as a guide to the rightness or wrongness of one's behavior.*

You are here because of the crimes (sins) you committed. You chose evil instead of good, wrong instead of right. And now there's no one to blame but yourself. But I'm not here to condemn you. I'm here to teach you that even if people don't forgive you, even if society does not forgive you, no matter the sin, no matter the crime. God will forgive you. He will forgive you through his son Jesus Christ. And when that happens, you can live in full freedom.

It wasn't until I got desperate for change, desperate for my life to be different, that I found the truth as to why my life was the way it was and how to change it. I gave my life to Jesus Christ and studied the Word of God, the Bible. Not only did I get free, but it changed the entire trajectory of my children's lives and their children's lives, my lineage going forward.

Okay, so if you think that this isn't for you… If you think that you're just going to get out and return to that same life that got you in here… If you think, oh, I'll just handle my drinking better… I'll go easier on the drugs… I'll just restrain myself from committing another crime… That's a false truth, that you believe, and it will not work. Another way of being in a metal prison is believing false truths. You have a belief in your mind that is false. What's the opposite of true? False, and again you must get your thinking right. You are not going to walk in true freedom unless you get help and make different decisions. Remember your decisions are what carves out your path in life. Accept the fact that you need help.

When you get back on the streets, you cannot drink or do drugs ever again.

You already did that, remember, that's why most of you are here. It's insane to think that you will be able to return to the same things again and not end up back in prison. Do you know what insanity means? To do the same thing over and over again expecting a different outcome.

You can't go back to hanging out with the same people in your life that aren't living right either. You won't be strong enough to resist temptation. If you really want a changed life, you'll have to work for it. There are no short cuts. You can't walk deep into the woods for 7 days and expect to get out in an hour. It takes time. You can't live most of your life the wrong way and expect it to change right away.

And you can be sure, if you go back to the same people, you were hanging out with before your incarceration, they'll be right there to offer you the bottle, the drugs, or an opportunity to make some quick money. Accept the fact that you need to make changes in your life.

Now, when I was in my place of hell. drinking and drugging and doing everything wrong, I hit my rock bottom. I wanted change and I was desperate. I was watching tv one day, flipping through the channels, and I heard this woman telling her story of being sexually abused as a child and how she found Jesus and he changed her entire life. He turned her life of horror into a life of blessing. Well, that's what I wanted. She told me that Jesus would meet me right where I was, full of sin, and living wrong. He would forgive all my sins and I could be free. Free from all the hurt, pain, and suffering. Free to live a life of peace and happiness. And I'm here to tell you that he did the same thing for me. Now, I want to help you get to that place in your life also. But first You need to Accept Jesus as your Savior.

I'm going to give you a quick teaching. There is a battle everyday between God and Satan, for your soul. That's it, in a nutshell. Now, for us to stay out of Satan's grip, God sent his son, Jesus, down to the earth to die for our sins. Jesus had to die a painful death. He had to be the offering. He had to take all our sins, curses, bear them all, and die on a cross for us. But after that God resurrected him from the dead and he now sits on the right hand of God. So now, whoever believes in him will be saved and receive all that he died for you to have. All you must do is accept him as your Lord and Savior.

Right now, God wants to save you. God is reaching out to you personally. Yes, you. I believe this is your divine appointment with God. Your second chance in life. He loves you and wants to help you change your life. He wants to give you another chance. All you must do is Accept that you are a sinner in need of a Savior.

To Receive Jesus as your Lord and Savior, pray this prayer:

"Dear Jesus, I know I'm a sinner,
I know I am not where I want to be,
and I want your forgiveness!
I believe that you died on the cross to pay the price for my sins.
Please wash me clean from all sin, shame, and guilt,
come into my life, Jesus, and be my Lord and Savior."

Jesus said, "You shall know the truth and the truth will make you free." John 8:32

Here are truths you need to get deep into your entire being:

- ✓ I must make great changes in my life, so I do not return to prison.

- ✓ I am 100% responsible for my life and all my decisions.

- ✓ I'm incarcerated because **I** made wrong decisions.

- ✓ Drugs and Alcohol use will carve me a path right back to prison.

- ✓ I need to be around people that live right.

- ✓ I need help. I cannot do this on my own.

Now, if you don't agree with everything in this chapter that you've read, then don't bother reading any further because it will not help you. You're not ready. You have not come to the end of yourself. Give the book to someone else or hold onto it until you're ready.

If you are in agreement with everything in this chapter, then let's move on to Chapter 2.

Chapter 2

REPENTANCE

Repentance – *Sincere regret or remorse.*

"I am sorry for the crimes I've committed."

Do you agree with that statement? Are you sorry? Truly sorry?

Or is that just the answer for the Judge or the parole board?

To repent in the Bible means to turn away from. So, when you commit a sin, you ask for forgiveness because you have sincere regret or remorse and then you repent. You turn away from. You do not do it again. Are you at that place?

If not, you must dig deep and ask yourself why? If you're in here for stealing, are you sorry for stealing? or do you think it wasn't a big deal, you were entitled, or have it justified some other way? The only way you're not going to come back to prison is if you are truly sorry for what you did and repent (turn away) from it, never doing it again. You own it. You admit it was wrong. There's no one to blame but yourself. You're not going to do it again. It was a bad decision, and you paid the price and learned the lesson. That's it.

Laws protect our safety and secure our rights as citizens. If it was not for laws, there would be utter chaos.

If you're the one breaking the law you're punished. If you're the victim, you're protected. How would you feel if the crime you serving time on right now, what if it was reversed? What if you were the victim and the crime was committed against you? You would want justice. You may call it revenge, but it's called justice. You can't escape laws whether it's God's laws or State and Federal laws. Even inmates have set up the laws that reign throughout the prison.

God set up the laws for the world. He gave us ten commandments:

1. You shall have no other gods before Me.

2. You shall not make idols.

3. You shall not take the name of the LORD your God in vain.

4. Remember the Sabbath day, to keep it holy.

5. Honor your father and your mother.

6. You shall not murder.

7. You shall not commit adultery.

8. You shall not steal.

9. You shall not bear false witness (Lie) against your neighbor.

10. You shall not covet anything that is thy neighbor's (Covet means lust or strong desire)

I always viewed the ten commandments as commandments from God that I must obey because God demanded it. It wasn't until I started teaching them to my daughter, that I discovered his real reason for the commandments. They are for our protection. When I said to her, "Thou shall not steal." she answered back, "I know why God said that, because he doesn't want anyone to steal from me." I just looked at her and read the next one. "Thou should not kill." And again, she answered, "I know that reason too, he doesn't want anyone to murder me." I was truly amazed. From that moment on I believe I looked at God differently. He wasn't a dictator; he was a loving father trying to protect his children. So now let's look at the commandments again from God's perspective.

1. You shall have no other gods before me. (So I can bless you)

2. You shall not make idols. (So I can bless you)

3. You shall not take the name of the LORD your God in vain. (So I can bless you)

4. Remember the Sabbath day, to keep it holy. (So you can receive my rest)

5. Honor your father and your mother. (So I can bless you)

6. You shall not murder. (I don't want anyone to murder you)

7. You shall not commit adultery. (I don't want anyone to betray you)

8. You shall not steal. (I don't want anyone to steal from you)

9. You shall not bear false witness (Lie) against your neighbor. (I don't want anyone to lie against you)

10. You shall not covet anything that is thy neighbor's (Covet means lust or strong desire) (I don't want anyone desiring what I've given to you)

Now we're at the place where you may begin to feel some discomfort. It's time to start confessing your sins to God. Going back to the memories that you may have tried to block out.

Now, when I did this, I went back as far as I could in my memory to remember the first time, I committed a sin. I thought of the memory of what I did, and asked God to forgive me. I did that over and over again, all the way to my present-day life. Every memory of sin I could think of. It took days, but when I was finished, it was like a huge weight had been lifted off my chest.

When God forgives your sin, he doesn't think about it again.

> *"For I will forgive their wickedness and will remember their sins no more." Hebrews 8:12*

Let's recap. God will forgive you of all your sins if you ask for forgiveness. He is just to forgive and even cleanses you from all unrighteousness. If you live God's way, you'll be blessed. Satan's way, cursed. God wants you to be happy and live a long, happy, life in freedom not confinement. Not punished and treated like an animal. Jesus Christ died for you to live an abundant life. Abundant means having plenty of. But you must choose that life for yourself and do the right thing.

> *The thief (Satan) cometh not, but for to steal, and to kill, and to destroy, I am come (Jesus) that they might have life, and that they might have it more abundantly. John 10:10*

Jesus said, "You shall know the truth and the truth will make you free." John 8:32

Here are truths you need to get deep into your entire being:

- ✓ I am truly sorry for all my sins.

- ✓ Nobody owes me anything, no matter how bad my life is or was.

- ✓ If something isn't mine, I cannot take it.

- ✓ I cannot go back to my old way of life.

- ✓ If I want to be free, I must confess my sins to God.

- ✓ I need help. I cannot do this on my own.

Now, if you don't agree with everything in this chapter that you've read, then don't bother reading any further because it will not help you. You're not ready. You have not come to the end of yourself. Give the book to someone else or hold onto it until you're ready.

If you are in agreement with everything in this chapter, then let's move on to Chapter 3.

Chapter 3

FORGIVENESS

So far, we've gone over acceptance, taking 100% ownership of what we did. Repentance, asking God to forgive us and then we repent (turn away) not repeating our same mistakes. Now we're at forgiveness.

The one we need forgiveness from the most, is God. And God has a law of forgiveness. He'll forgive all that you've done, because of his son Jesus's sacrifice, only if you forgive all those who sinned against you.

> **But if you do not forgive men their sins, your father will not forgive your sins. Matthew 6:15**

For most of us, this is the hardest part of the journey. See once again Satan tries to keep you in unforgiveness because unforgiveness fuels anger, rage, pride, bitterness, and resentment which keeps you in bondage and leads you to greater sins, like murder. The secret of forgiveness, and the reason God demands it, is once again for our benefit.

Unforgiveness creates an inner prison inside of us. We live in an emotional prison living in constant misery and upset which causes us to use alcohol and drugs just to cope. Trying to find some kind of false happiness or peace. It's all just an evil trap to keep you stuck. The worst part is, as you go over this in your mind and relive every negative emotion from the event, chances are the person or people that did this to you, aren't giving it another thought. So, they get you again.

So, what do we do? How do you forgive? Well first, forgiveness is not a feeling, it's a decision. You can't wait until you feel like forgiving because that feeling may not ever come. You need to make the decision to forgive, so you stay free. Don't let them get you again, leading you right back to prison. And forgiveness does not by any means say that the person that wronged you is getting away with anything. One thing I have learned in my life, If I forgive the person that wronged me and don't take it into my own hands, God vindicates me. And believe me you do not want to be on God's bad side.

Now when you give the situation to God, he'll take care of it, that way you can stay free and in peace. It's quite a mental battle though. Satan will constantly try to bring your mind to what that person did to you, but don't be tempted. Just say no, I have forgiven that person and set your mind on something else.

Let's do an exercise, close your eyes, and go to that place in your memory where someone wronged you or hurt you. I want you to pray this prayer. God, you know the hardest part of our walk down here is getting along with others and forgiving them. Right now, I need your assistance, your divine help. Help me to forgive this person {name the person) and not only forgive but forget. I want to be free. In Jesus name, amen.

You must have practical ways of dealing with this too. Whenever these memories come up you must do something to distract your mind and bring yourself back to the present. Remind yourself, you can't seek revenge, or you'll go back to prison and guess what, they got you again. Remember, every time you let that unforgiveness take over, they win, not you. Find ways to not think about it. Go workout, run it off, call a friend, pray. Always stay away from that person. Do not engage with them in anyway. Nothing good will ever come from it. Don't let unforgiveness take your freedom away. Always come back to the truth that you must forgive them for YOUR peace and freedom.

FORGIVENESS PART TWO

Now, what do you do when you are the one that needs to be forgiven? The first thing you must do is respect that person's wishes. You can ask them to forgive you but if they do not want to re-relationship with you, you must respect that.

If it's a spouse or child, it's very difficult. The child, I have seen, is angry at you for not being around. They don't want to invest the time with you hoping that you'll stay in their life this time, and then you're gone again. It's a protective method. However, I have seen if you give them space, but keep letting them know that you want to be in their life, the child tends to come around. I would recommend counseling to help that relationship.

If you want the person back that you have wronged, in your life, pray to God and ask him to forgive you, if you haven't already. Next, ask God to soften that person's heart to forgive you. But again, I must reiterate, it's a long process and you must respect whether the person you have wronged, wants you in his or her life again.

Let me give you an example. What if you were the victim. Your friend, whom you trust, comes over to hang out. You leave the room for a minute. You come back and visit with your friend for a while. He leaves and later you notice your wallet is missing. Your upset, you call your friend, he denies taking your wallet. You find out for sure that he has stolen your wallet. He then calls and apologizes. Now, the next time he's at your house, if you ever allow him to be, are you going to leave your wallet on the table? My guess is no. It will take a while to be able to trust him again.

FORGIVENESS

People need time to trust again, and you must prove your sincerity. That's the consequence of breaking trust. So, while you're waiting on people to trust you, put your focus on something you can control, like building yourself a better life.

> *Jesus said, "You shall know the truth and the truth will make you free." John 8:32*

Here are truths you need to get deep into your entire being:

- ✓ In order for God to forgive me, I must forgive others.

- ✓ In order to be free, I must forgive others.

- ✓ Unforgiveness will keep me imprisoned.

- ✓ Unforgiveness is like drinking poison and expecting the other person to die.

- ✓ Unforgiveness is like drinking poison, it causes sickness and disease.

- ✓ I need help. I cannot do this on my own.

Now, if you don't agree with everything in this chapter that you've read, then don't bother reading any further because it will not help you. You're not ready. You have not come to the end of yourself. Give the book to someone else or hold onto it until you're ready.

If you are in agreement with everything in this chapter, then let's move on to Chapter 4.

Chapter 4
HEALING YOUR SOUL

After the forgiveness process, we need healing. And I say we because this is a process, we all must do. It's not just for prisoners. It's for all of us sinners and all of us that are hurting.

Your soul is your mind, will, and emotions. If your soul is full of junk, like we talked about, you must repent first then you need God to heal you. Soul wounds are the past emotional injuries that manifest by giving us wrong attitudes and identities.

Let's talk about anger. Are you angry all the time? Or maybe the slightest thing makes you angry? Anger is usually a sign that you have a soul wound of fear or you're living in unforgiveness. A soul wound can also be brought on by trauma. So, your anger can be a result of fear of that trauma happening again. It's up to you to do the digging, getting to the root issue, and forgive if needed. Next comes healing.

God has designed our body to heal on its own. Think about it, if you cut your finger, it will heal without you having to do anything. A larger cut may scab over and eventually heal, but if you keep picking at that scab and reopening the wound, it will never heal.

Let me tell you one of my deepest soul wounds. My father left us all when I was 14 years old and never came back, to this day. When he announced to us 4 kids, that he was leaving, we were all upset. I was heartbroken, wrecked, scared. "Who's going to take care of us now?" "Who's going to provide for us now?" "Who's going to protect us? My father was a strong, street fighter. He was also the disciplinary of the house. When he left, I remember saying, "Good, I'll never have to listen to another person again." So instead of being hurt, I chose anger, it was a coping method. This anger led me to rebellion, which led to years and years of hell and hardships.

Now, let me ask you a question, if you could have anything in this life, what would you choose? For most the answer would be money, power, but the real answer should be peace. Peace is what your soul and body craves. Peace allows you to have more self-control and self-control is powerful. You see everyone in prison has lived their lives without self-control. They lived by the emotions they felt. Angry, entitled, addicted, fearful. The list goes on and on. That's another reason you want to forgive and heal so you can have peace which leads to self-control which leads to a life of freedom.

So, let's get your soul healed. For this, I want you to close your eyes. Let's just start with one event that your mind plays over and over again. Now first forgive that person or ask God for forgiveness if you were the one who caused it. Pray this prayer. "God, this event in my life has caused me so much hurt, anger, and pain. Please forgive me for my part. I ask you to heal me and free me from the soul wounds it brought into my life. Please free me from this pain. In Jesus name, amen."

Here's something you may not know. The human mind does not know the difference between real and imagination. When you've gone through a trauma and you start reliving it in your memory, your mind thinks it is happening again. That's why your body goes through those same emotions, tensing up, the burning in your chest, the anger. You must let it go.

Jesus said, "You shall know the truth and the truth will make you free." John 8:32

Here are truths you need to get deep into your entire being:

- ✓ I need to receive healing from God for my soul wounds.

- ✓ Sometimes people are only in my life for a reason or a season.

- ✓ Hurting people, hurt people

- ✓ People are put in your life by God or by Satan.

- ✓ The battle every day is between God and Satan for your soul.

- ✓ I need to seek healing.

Now, if you don't agree with everything in this chapter that you've read, then don't bother reading any further because it will not help you. You're not ready. You have not come to the end of yourself. Give the book to someone else or hold onto it until you're ready.

If you are in agreement with everything in this chapter, then let's move on to Chapter 5.

Chapter 5

FREEDOM

Everyone wants freedom. Freedom can be defined in a number of ways but the freedom definition I want to talk about in this chapter is:

> **Freedom** – The state of not being imprisoned or enslaved.

So, we talked about freedom from mental and physical prisons but notice the other word in the definition, enslaved. Slavery no longer exists in America, thank God, but people are still enslaved. That is to sin…To addictions…To fear…To anger… it goes on and on.

How does this happen? Falling into sin. When you keep choosing sin over doing what's right, you eventually become enslaved. Former addicts will tell you, first I only did drugs on the weekend and had it under control. But then I wanted to do drugs more and more and before I knew it, it had a hold on me. I couldn't stop. The addict became enslaved to the drug.

> **Addiction** – A condition in which a person is unable to stop using a substance or engaging in a behavior.

Addiction can be found in the bible defined as a strong hold. And that's what an addiction is, a strong hold upon you. Not only did we sin against God, but now we've become enslaved to our sin.

> **Jesus replied, "I tell you the truth, everyone who sins is a slave of sin." John 8:34**

Now, I'm living proof, a testimony to overcoming addictions. I was addicted to drugs, alcohol, even cigarettes and the Lord delivered me from them all. How? Well first I had to start digging down to the root of my addiction. Why did I drink every night until I passed out? Because I hated how my life was. I was escaping all my abandonment issues from my father, and all the abuse, hurt, and pain, I managed to pick up along my life's journey.

Next, I asked myself, is this really helping me? No, it's making everything worse. I have even more problems now after making worse decisions in a drunken, drugged out state.

I then had to ask myself, Do I want my life to change? Or am I ready to die and continue the path that I'm on. I had to make the decision, yes, I want my life to change, and I had to commit to it, no matter how hard it was at times.

Finally, I had to pray to Jesus to help me. I knew I couldn't do it on my own. I already proved that. It is Jesus who sets you free. He tells us in the Bible.

"Who the son sets free is free indeed." John 8:36

The truth for me was drugs and alcohol did not make anything better for me. Yes, it was fun and games for a little while but then I became enslaved and miserable. So, once I confessed my sins, my addictions, and I found the truth and made up my mind to stop, Jesus set me free. It's been about 25 years.

Now, I had to do things in the practical way of living too. Sometimes God will deliver you immediately and sometimes it's a walk to get out. Now for me the drugs were easier than the alcohol. The alcohol had a stronger grip and took work. I had to make big changes in my life. I had to sever ties with certain friends, not go into a bar ever, not drink at all. Cold turkey. But whenever I was at a weak point the good Lord gave me the strength to stay sober. For those of you with drug and alcohol addictions, think of how much time you've wasted. Nothing good or productive came out of it. It's like you did time on the outside too. How many relationships has your addiction ruined? Spouses, children, parents, siblings, loved ones? Your addiction certainly affected them too.

Let's get you free now. Hopefully you've all managed to stay sober while you were here in prison. But I know there are drugs and alcohol in prisons also. So, let's begin by accepting that you need to be free and to let go of your addictions. You'll have to do the work and dig down to the root of the problem. But right now, those who want to be free, let's pray to Jesus to help us.

Jesus, you died on the cross for me and took away all power from the devil. I'm coming to you today. Asking you to deliver me from my addictions. I want to be free, but I need your help. Help me to be strong and resist temptation. Help me to become free and stay free. Help me fight this battle. In your name Jesus I pray, amen.

Jesus said, "You shall know the truth and the truth will make you free." John 8:32

Here are truths you need to get deep into your entire being:

- ✓ If I continue to choose sin, I will become enslaved.

- ✓ For my life to be different, I must make different decisions.

- ✓ I must make big changes in my life to be free.

- ✓ I cannot be around people that aren't living right.

- ✓ I cannot be in certain places or situations that will tempt me to sin.

- ✓ I cannot do this on my own. I need help.

Great! You made it to the end of the book. I'm so glad. I pray that this book has equipped you to begin your journey to true freedom.

Just remember, in your journey, if you trip up and find yourself falling back into sin… Quickly get back up! It's not the falling that causes us to fail. It's the staying down and not getting back up. Like the old saying goes, if you fall off the horse, get right back on.

May God bless you and keep you in true freedom!

Kim Cornell

www.ingramcontent.com/pod-product-compliance
Lightning Source LLC
LaVergne TN
LVHW021742060526
838200LV00052B/3423